Favorite Pets

Dogs

by Christina Leaf

BELLWETHER MEDIA
MINNEAPOLIS, MN

Blastoff! Beginners are developed by literacy experts and educators to meet the needs of early readers. These engaging informational texts support young children as they begin reading about their world. Through simple language and high frequency words paired with crisp, colorful photos, Blastoff! Beginners launch young readers into the universe of independent reading.

Blastoff! Universe

Reading Level — Grade K — Grades 1-3 — Grade 4

Sight Words in This Book 🔍

a	get	little	some	this
are	good	many	the	to
big	here	of	their	
can	how	on	them	
eat	is	one	there	
from	like	play	they	

This edition first published in 2021 by Bellwether Media, Inc.

No part of this publication may be reproduced in whole or in part without written permission of the publisher. For information regarding permission, write to Bellwether Media, Inc., Attention: Permissions Department, 6012 Blue Circle Drive, Minnetonka, MN 55343.

Library of Congress Cataloging-in-Publication Data

Names: Leaf, Christina, author.
Title: Dogs / by Christina Leaf.
Description: Minneapolis, MN : Bellwether Media, Inc., 2021. | Series: Favorite pets |
    Includes bibliographical references and index. | Audience: Grades K-1
Identifiers: LCCN 2020007075 (print) | LCCN 2020007076 (ebook) | ISBN 9781644873144 (library binding) |
    ISBN 9781681038018 (paperback) | ISBN 9781681037776 (ebook)
Subjects: LCSH: Dogs--Juvenile literature. | Pets--Juvenile literature.
Classification: LCC SF426.5 .L44 2021 (print) | LCC SF426.5 (ebook) | DDC 636.7--dc23
LC record available at https://lccn.loc.gov/2020007075
LC ebook record available at https://lccn.loc.gov/2020007076

Editor: Amy McDonald   Designer: Jeffrey Kollock

Printed in the United States of America, North Mankato, MN.

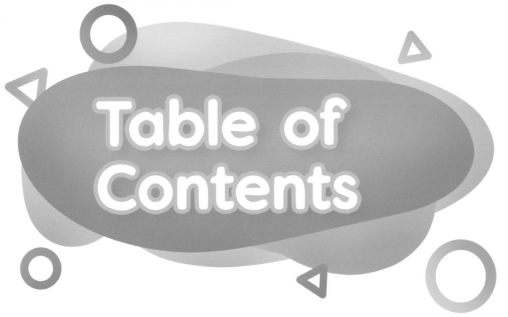

Table of Contents

Pet Dogs!

Tug! Fetch!
Shake!
Pet dogs
like to play!

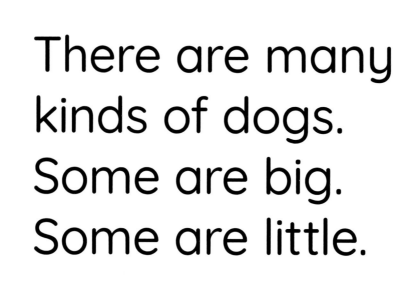

There are many
kinds of dogs.
Some are big.
Some are little.

French
bulldog

Labrador retriever

Great Dane

Care

Dogs eat
from dishes.
They like **kibbles**
or canned food.

kibbles

dish

Dogs need walks. **Owners** take them on a **leash**.

leash

owner

Owners
brush dogs.
This keeps
their fur clean.

brushing

Dogs get sick. Owners bring dogs to the **vet**.

vet

15

Life with Dogs

Dogs keep watch.
They bark.
Someone is here!

barking

Dogs wag their tails. This shows how they feel.

Dogs learn tricks.
This one can fetch.
Good dog!

Dog Facts

Pet Dog Supplies

bed

toys

food and
water dishes

leash

Dog Toys

tennis ball

rope toy

squeak
toy

Glossary

kibbles

small, dry pieces of food

leash

a line or rope for holding dogs

owners

people who care for dogs

vet

a doctor for animals

To Learn More

ON THE WEB

FACTSURFER

Factsurfer.com gives you a safe, fun way to find more information.

1. Go to www.factsurfer.com.

2. Enter "pet dogs" into the search box and click 🔍.

3. Select your book cover to see a list of related content.

Index